DO IT

SRISHTI WADHWA

To everyone who inspired me, in someway or another.

Contents

Preface

I am so glad that you are reading this book right now. It took me almost two years to write it and finally it's finished. I love writing self-help content, at first I started out by writing blogs on my website but I knew I had to do more. That's when I decided to write this book. Like I said it took two years to write, believe me, it was tedious. There were so many moments where I felt like giving up, but I kept going. Also for everyone who is wondering, how can I write a self-help book at 17? Well to be honest I feel like our experience comes from observance rather than our age. Although, our age is a contributing factor, but it matters only to an extent.

This book contains a complete roadmap of following your passion. It includes all the important steps you need to keep in mind while aiming for success in life. I tried to include every crucial step that is going to be useful in your journey. Every point has been added after intense consideration. I really think you are going to love this book. Before reading, please keep in mind, everything I have mentioned in this book is based on real life, I actually apply most of these things in my life and following them gave me pretty amazing results. I hope you will follow these suggestions and I know they will be life changing.

To be honest, implementing new habits in life can be challenging. I know it takes a lot of courage to do something beyond your comfort zone. According to me, you cannot achieve success unless you decide to break your bubble, it might intimidate you, but it will open a new world to you- a world that is untouched and full of opportunities. I know this book is a powerful tool you need to break out of your bubble, so, make good use of it.

About The Author

My name is Srishti Wadhwa. I don't know what to write because there are so many things that I want to share about myself. But I can't mention them all. So let's start with the basics. I am 17. I love writing, singing, painting, and exercising, that's right! Lately I have become a fitness freak, although I haven't seen any promising results yet. Don't worry, I am not quitting exercising anytime soon, afterall it is all about consistency.

I started writing two years back, I never really thought I would publish a book someday. 7th grade Srishti would be so proud to see how far she has come. I always used to think writing is not my cup of tea, until I actually tried writing for the first time. It might seem all glitter and gold but its not true. Everything I have achieved in my life is a result of sheer hardwork, numerous sleepless nights and a ton of blood and sweat. It might seem like a dialogue straight out of Bollywood movie but it's true. Although, I do want to mention that I am nowhere near my ultimate goal. It's a long, tiring, and tedious process and I am ready to explore what life has to offer in coming years. Infact, I am so excited to see what future holds for me, I hope it's something good.

The idea behind this book was a 'go-to person who's there to give you advise' I wanted to write this book in such a way, that every time you come across a problem you should be able to overcome it through this book. I really hope this book answers all your questions. So are you ready to begin the race? I promise I'll cheer for you all the way. Let's go and win this thing.

HAPPY READING!

CHAPTER ONE

EXPLORE YOURSELF

Well first things first, I want to tell you that success have different meanings for different
people, it could be anything ranging from getting into your dream university or getting a job
that you always wanting to have.
But to achieve that success you should know, what you are aiming for and this is the most
important step that goes in the making of a successful life.
There are basically two ways by which you can know what your passion/interest/dream/goal
is.

The first is a bit simple and short. So all you have to do is take a seat, take a deep breath, close your eyes and think what will really keep you awake till two in the night. What is that one thing in which you could put all your heart and soul? And you can fight anyone to achieve that. Also make sure not to include anything just for the motive of earning money.

If you got your answer by now, well congrats you now know what you truly love and want to achieve from the bottom of your heart. And if you are a bit confused or maybe completely blank. Just don't worry I am here to back you. Just try out the second way. Also the second one could be a bit lengthy before you can get your answer but I am sure it's going to be worth it.

The second way says, to find your passion I would recommend to try different things out, like you could maybe try singing, who knows maybe you could be the next Shawn Mendes or Taylor Swift and it's okay if you are not good at it just move on and try dancing, again if you found that you are not good at it, move on try athletics and just keep going on like this until you can find that one particular thing.

One piece of advice here is just please don't assume that you are not good at this particular thing because you weren't able to do it in the past. Something very similar happened with me and I have now tried to learn from my mistake

"This goes back to when I was in sixth grade, my writing skills were horrible, like literally horrible is the word, I use to write my essays like a first grader and that's just when I assumed I could never be able to write in my whole life, and that's where all these things went wrong. The situation went even worse in seventh and eighth grade. In my exams I used to do well in my literature section but when it came to writing section, it was because of this section my entire percentage went down, there was not much improvement in my freshman year but when I came into my sophomore year things changed because it was the first time ever I tried writing not just for the sake of completing my writing section in my exam, but for real. And this time I figured I was just living in this world of illusion when actually that skill was inside me and this time I embraced it."

If there is one thing that I could tell my younger self it would be that hey! Just try to embrace what you have in yourself, I know you have that capability. But at least try.

And now you guys know why I said just don't assume anything just because you have never tried it in your whole life, maybe that thing is just made for you.

I brought this topic of exploring yourself first because you cannot achieve anything until you know what you are aiming for. Moreover your passion is a blessing to you which can actually turn your life upside down, and it's great to have one right inside you, waiting for you to let it out and show the world what you are capable of.

Also, try to be as creative as you can while you are on your exploration journey. And I know at the end you are going to find out what you truly love, so keep these two methods in your mind and work accordingly.

CHAPTER TWO

FOLLOW YOUR INTEREST

Now that you have known what your passion/interest is. It's now time to move on to our second step which is to actually follow it. Now I know there are some of you guys out there who know what their dream is but are still manipulated to follow some other one, or maybe not doing it because they might be afraid of what society will say or maybe their parents are not allowing them to achieve/do that.

Now let's take up each of these situations one by one because I truly want you to do what you love and not what other people expect from you.

First situation is when you are not following your interests because you are afraid of what society/your neighbors/relatives will say.

Now, you might have heard a lot of people talking about this "Do what you love, Follow your heart..."

But our generation is still being judged by our society who does not leave a single chance of talking trash behind our back.

Let me tell you, if you are aiming to achieve something, you should know that people are going to back you, they are going to criticize you even if you are absolutely happy with what you are doing.

Just like the work of an artist is to draw, the work of a singer is to sing, similarly the job of criticizing is given to our society. You just have to accept this fact and keep moving on. Don't care what people are going to say about you because you have only one single life and try living it to the fullest.

Believe me no one is even going to care even if you are dying, so why care about their stupid judgments.

Let me tell you guys a real life experience that changed the way of my thinking

"I was about 13 years old and I was at my cousin's sister's house. I was super excited to go to the newly constructed park nearby. I went there with my little brother who was about 7 at that time. I was playing on one of the swings and then suddenly one of my fingers got stuck under the swing. I called my brother to help me out because the swing was heavy. Moreover, my hand was completely numb and I wasn't able to move it at all. Luckily I finally got my finger out and the blood was flowing like melting ice. I rushed towards my cousin's home and I found a couple of people on the street, minding their business even when they saw a girl crying while her whole hand was covered in blood and no one literally cared to ask me what actually happened, and just forgot about even helping me. Hopefully I am fine now and my finger too."

But the incident that day actually taught me the lesson I just mentioned earlier. That's when I decided to not give society even the slightest chance of interfering in my decision making process.

And now you guys now know what to do if you ever get a thought of not doing something that you love because people will be judging you. Just think of my story and don't let them rule over your mind.

With this now let's move on to something serious which is when your parents are not allowing you to achieve/do something you love

I know we are living in the 21st century where most of the parents do understand and respect what their kids want to do, but still there are exceptions and let's talk about how you can actually persuade your parents so that they can respect your decisions.

First, if you are a parent and you are reading, it is important for you to interact with your kids because it would make a lot of difference and communication is the only way that can make a relationship better. As a parent you should understand what your kids really want and you guys should let them be independent and let them make their own decisions. Now I know that I am no one who could actually give you guys parenting advice but still these would be the things that I want my parents to do, to improve that communication gap.

Secondly, if you are stuck in a situation where your parents are not so happy with what your dream is. For example, you might want to move abroad for college or a job, you might want to become an investor which they think is risky, or you might want to work in the film industry which according to them is not safe/morally right... There are so many that I can think of right now but it is not possible to mention them right here.

All you have to do is make them understand that this is something that is going to make me happy. I could possibly have a much better future and a life full of inner satisfaction.

I know you guys might think that your parents might be too strict to understand this. But try giving it a shot and I know it's going to be worth it. Like actually what do you think could have been the reason that your parents still have not been able to actually know what you truly love. It's because you never tried telling them, right? Now actually for the first time give it a shot and after this they are definitely going to support you.

Now that we have actually got to know how to clear the obstacle that comes in the way of our "following your passion journey" it's now time to actually plan things out.

CHAPTER THREE

PLANNING

Now planning is a great way by which you can be on track and keep running like a bullet train. It's always better to plan things out before actually doing them. Even doing small things like being in the habit of writing your to-do list everyday could be very effective.

There are basically two types of planning according to me- daily/short term planning and long term planning

Let's talk about both of them one by one –

Daily/Short Term Planning

You don't need any fancy planner to start writing what your goal is. Any normal notebook or even a notepad will work perfectly. It's just that you have to be persistent since persistence is the key to success.

Now let me tell you guys how you can actually start planning each and every day.

Seems simple but it is not. First, start writing what your goal is for each and every day. Just make it a part of your morning routine. After you jot down all the points, keep them as the goal of your day and the deadline is before you go to sleep. Now write the same points on a sticky note and stick it at a place where you can see it every time you pass by. I would suggest you stick it on your fridge or any other wall of your house/dorm/office.

Now you might be thinking that I might have gone crazy. Like what in the world am I telling you guys to do? So the reason behind why I told you guys to write your goal so that you can challenge yourself every day. And I told you to paste the same on your wall/fridge so that every time you pass by you can actually get a reminder that you still have to do a few things to call it a day off and make it meaningful.

Also whenever you complete a task tick that up because after all it's an achievement. From now on tell yourself that you have to ask a few questions to yourself before going to sleep and do it without fail. The questions are mentioned below-

- Would I call it a day?

- Am I satisfied with all the things I have done today?
- Did I actually do something today so that it can help me in reaching my ultimate goal?
- List the three things/lessons I learned today?

If your answers to all the questions are affirmative you are doing great. And if not, it's okay even though it took me one and a half months before I started getting affirmative answers more regularly. There are going to be days where you will feel like doing nothing and it's okay, but at the end of the day you, yourself will feel motivated after not seeing all those ticks on your list.

And there will be a voice in your head saying that- I am going to do this thing and I can, because "it is in my blood", I guess I love Shawn Mendes.

But if you still feel that you are not able to stay motivated, stay tuned since there is a topic of how to stay motivated that is going to come further.

Daily planning is great in the long run as it helps you to be prepared for your ultimate goal and to achieve that. It's more like taking baby steps before you actually take the real ones.

Now since we have talked about daily planning let's move to our second planning i.e. Long term planning

As the name suggests it's quite understandable that we use this planning to plan big things and major events that are going to occur in the future but since they are big you have to start planning early.

Like maybe you have to apply to college abroad next year you are going to plan your SAT/ ACT, essays, extracurricular, list of colleges you will consider applying to. Of course you cannot do all of this before the night before the deadline.

Or maybe you are planning to buy a house. You have to start preparing two-three years prior and clear all your payments if you want the bank to pass your loan.

Also if you want to achieve something big, list down the major stepping stones you need to pass in order to win the race. And keep a track so that you can actually get a fair idea of what it will take to be where you truly want to.

Okay let's take a break go and grab a sheet of paper and a pen. Write down the things that you would love yourself achieving in the next year. Write that and as we are going to move forward I know you are able to achieve everything mentioned on that list.

Since we are about to move on to our next topic there is one last thing that I would love to mention which is that I know that you would do great

CHAPTER FOUR

KNOW YOUR INTEREST/GOAL

So since we have already talked about the three most important things that take into making a successful goal, it's now time to move on to our next important step which is knowing your interests better.

Now, I might have helped you in finding out what your passion is, thus it becomes my moral duty to take you to your ultimate goal. If we both have started this together then we are also going to end this journey together without fail.

You are also going to agree what I am about to say right now-

Just because you love doing something doesn't mean that you have a full knowledge about your goal. It is so important to know more about what you are aiming for. I can actually write a book on 21 ways to know your goal better but for now let's talk about it in brief.

Okay let's understand this with an example –

Suppose you are a Kathak (a form of classical dance) dancer and you are just about to perform on the stage and maybe you are not familiar with the Taal (beats) of performing a salami (a short dance which ends with a salaam/greeting pose). Do you think that you are going to end up giving a mesmerizing performance? Well I think you know the answer yourself. Now first let me give the answer to the question that might be revolving around your mind. How do I know so much about kathak? It's because I am a kathak dancer and I know how you feel just before performing on the stage. I have been through that.

Now I guess we might have gone a little off from where we actually started. I gave the example so that it can be more relatable to you guys that knowing something just by name doesn't mean you know the depths of it. If you want to achieve something try knowing more and more things about it, so that you could possibly know every bit and piece of your interest.

Ex-

- If you want to become a singer try singing different notes or maybe keep a check on who won the Grammy this year, was it your favorite singer? Doing this can actually give you an idea of which type of music people love hearing and you can give them that content.

- If you want to become a fashion blogger try learning new styles, maybe you can keep a check on red carpets all over the world, see which outfit you love the most from the Met Gala this year. This can possibly help you to innovate new ideas and create your own fashion.

- If you want to get into your dream university, know how you can actually write stellar essays and learn the skill of making your application absolutely different from others. This can possibly increase your chances of getting in.

Now there are literally so many passions and interests that I can possibly talk about but then this book is going to be never ending.

So let me tell you what I actually meant while stating all these examples-

Your passion is vulnerable and there is so much that you can know about it. And you don't need any counselors or advisors to guide you out. There is literally so much information that is out in the world-so many books, newspapers, articles, videos, in fact the whole internet is full of so many things that if you once step out in, there is no end to it.

So by reading all this, I am pretty sure now you know, without knowing your interest you are a fish without water. If you have to survive then know how to avail yourself with water.

CHAPTER FIVE

TIME MANAGEMENT

Now let's talk about time management, one of the most important factors that almost everyone talks about.

So I know you guys might have heard the famous saying i.e. time is precious and vulnerable, time is money, time waits for no one. Now why do people actually say this?

Is time really that precious? Well to find out the answer stick with me up till the end. In this topic I am going to answer so many questions revolving around your mind related to time management. I have discussed planning earlier but this is completely opposite of that. Planning out your day doesn't mean you are able to manage your time. So let's start.

I remember when I was in my sixth grade, I had an essay to write on time is precious and I am not even kidding but I actually remember the starting line that I used in that essay which said-

Just like we cannot put together the flower that has been plucked from the plant, just like we cannot take back what we have said once. Similarly, once time has gone , it never comes back.

Since it is a translation of Hindi it might sound a bit weird. But let's quickly try to grasp the lesson with an example.

Have you ever been disappointed and said, oh! Boy, I could have worked harder when I had all that time with me. I know there might have been a situation in the lives of everyone reading this right now and its human behavior.

We humans always leave our self-regret afterwards and we can actually see that failure coming but still we continue to waste our time.

Maybe you have an exam tomorrow and you are continuously scrolling on your social media account and then suddenly it comes to your mind that, what are you doing STUDY or you will score horrible. But then the other side of us says that it doesn't really matter if I will score one or two marks less.

But then on our result day seeing those poor marks in our hands made us realize that we should have studied then. We had already seen those poor marks coming but we were so busy scrolling through our social media pages that we couldn't help ourselves out.

Now is there a cure to it? Well the answer is yes! Absolutely.

I am actually going to guide you on how you can actually make your 24 hours' worth it.

First I know most of us have tried making time tables but unfortunately we were not able to walk on it. Instead of writing it out, start thinking it out.

Sounds weird but it's not. So from now onwards before falling asleep think about what are all those things that you will put on your to-do list. Got it, great!

Start out by visualizing your whole entire day everything from waking up to doing your favorite thing in the day and while eating meals. Now if you are done visualizing try following it out like actually.

This is a small step by which you can actually help you save a lot of time thinking what to do next. Now the reason why those written time tables aren't of much help is because each of our days are different with different goals and objectives. And there are weekends too where you have to enjoy but you cannot do that while following our old traditional written time table, which leaves us no choice except for breaking the sequence or completely doing our own things out. That's the reason why you should try planning out the sequence of doing things in a particular order beforehand since it helps you to save some precious hours that you can utilize elsewhere.

Now there is one relatable example which I think is the best because it's common to us all

So have you ever realized that feeling of precious time when the last 5 minutes of your exam are left out and you don't even have the time to blink your eyes properly? Now if we all would start valuing time like that don't you think that we all will end up being Einstein or maybe do a wonderful discovery?

Well if that would be the case life would be so much different. We always take some things in our lives for granted. Now if I am going to tell you that the earth is going to be destroyed in one hour. What will we all do? Probably meeting up our nears and dears or doing the things that we have only dreamt of doing. Right? So why not right now.

That's when this topic of time management comes in. That day when the feeling of utilizing our time better will come from our heart, there will be no one who can actually stop us from achieving what we actually want.

I guess now you all have the answer to the question I asked in the begging which said-

Is time really that precious? Yes, it is.

Now before moving to the next topic I would say that, respect time because it is the best teacher in the entire universe. No one can teach you things that time can.

CHAPTER SIX

STAY MOTIVATED

Remember when I told you that I would be talking about staying motivated later in the book well now I guess it is the time.

Now I know everyone out there reading this this right now must have felt this way at some point of their life-

You know what you want, you know what your aim is, and you want to achieve it so badly but still you are not feeling motivated enough to start working for it.

First things first, after reading this there might be a question revolving around your mind, is there a cure to it? How can we feel motivated?

Yes there is a cure and yes you can feel motivated. So if you want to know how, keep reading and if there is something that you will take after this book let it be this.

Who do you think decides if we are feeling motivated or not. Our brain, I am sorry to say but our brain is the one who plays games with us.

And once if we will learn how to tackle our brain, let me tell you no one can actually stop you fr

om being successful and achieving that.

Let me explain with an example,

Suppose you are ready to study because you know you have an exam tomorrow but when you opened up your book you suddenly start thinking about some incident which is not even related to it but then when you stop thinking you got to know that you officially wasted one hour.

So in this case your mind deliberately put that stuff in front of you and you started thinking about it.

So from now onwards whenever something like this happens tell your brain, a big "NO" that I don't want to think about some random random incident right now, rather I would appreciate you to be focused.

It might sound absurd but believe me it's not, I know you might say that the brain is the one who controls our entire body, feeling and emotions so how can I control my brain?

Yes that's true but you can control your brain, well you might have listened to that voice that comes from within you which warns you of any danger. That same voice will stop your brain. That voice is your soul.

Now I know some you might not have understood this thing but for the ones who did, congrats.

So for the ones who didn't understand, let me tell you one more way because after all I promised you that I am going to be there till the end of our journey of success.

Now this method is a general one and the ironic thing is, in this way we are actually going to force our brain to think of incidents.

Let us consider this with the same example to make things much more clear-

Suppose you have an exam tomorrow but you are not feeling motivated enough to study. Then close your eyes and take a deep breath and think of the result (positive) that you are expecting.

Which means in this case you think that you have scored full marks in the exam you are preparing for and therefore your brain will automatically think of working hard to achieve that.

Let's take another example-

If you are aiming to get into your dream university and not feeling motivated to work for it anymore, think that it's your moving day and you are there in your dorm, isn't that motivating, yes it is indeed.

Now like I told you that your brain is the one that plays games but here you will force it to think of positive results and it will automatically help you to work hard.

Now I discussed two ways to feel motivated and both of them were completely opposite to each other, in the first one we tried to control our thoughts and be dominant over our brain. But in the second way we learn how to manipulate our brain so that it can see what we want it to see and ultimately we can achieve success.

Now to be honest the second way works perfectly for me and I have been trying it out for a very long time now. And I hope it's going to work for you as well. Now as I told you that we still have a long way to reach our ultimate goal and I know you can do this because you actually deserve to be there. Work from all your heart, put all your blood and sweat in it, just so there are no regressions afterwards. Remember we can do this together. Now before moving on to the next step I would say, stay motivated and stay hydrated.

CHAPTER SEVEN

TAKE CHALLENGES

Well the next important step that we have to keep in mind while we are aiming for success is to keep taking challenges at every point of our life.

Challenges not only make us feel confident but are actually a great way of keeping a check on our progress. Now there are numerous ways of taking challenges in our path of success.

Now you might think why is there a need to take challenges when we already have so much to think and do. Well like always let's discuss this out

Now first answer my question, how do you think you can define a challenge. Now take a break, think and come back.

Done. Well let me guess what your answer was. I think most of you might have defined challenges like hurdles in our path, testing our skills out by taking part in various competitions, Olympiads, or maybe doing something out of your comfort zone, which is true to some extent.

It doesn't really matter what your answer was but I actually define challenge as, "a phase of life different from others, which leaves you with so much experience." And this is the phase where you can learn so much from. Challenges are the second most important teacher after time.

Now taking challenges does not always have to be necessarily in the form of competitions.

Let's understand this with an example-

Suppose you are aiming to wake up early in the morning to be extra productive now this is also a challenge like I said, going out of your comfort zone is a challenge.

And if you succeed in waking up early, first of all congrats but do you know, what would be the experience you will grab from this phase? It will be how you managed to be extra productive that day, and this experience is one which you usually don't get to know regularly.

I guess now you know why I defined challenges like that.

Also like some of you might guess, challenges such as taking part in various competitions etc. to test your skill. Well you can always try out that because it will also give you a lot of experience related to your field.

Now I guess we have the answer to the question that I asked you guys out earlier, regarding why we should take challenges. Let me give you a few reasons to make you believe that they are there to spice up our lives.

Well I know this is one most common thing that we all might have thought about at some point of our life. We all wish to have a life without challenges and it's ironic because I am telling you guys to take more of them.

Now like I mentioned earlier, challenges make us feel much more experienced and tough not only mentally but physically as well.

I know that it might have made you believe a little bit, but if you still are not convinced try doing something out of your comfort zone once and you yourself will feel proud to be able to do that. And ultimately it will help you in taking more of those.

Now I guess that's the end for this topic. Also don't be afraid of taking challenges, they will help you to flourish.

Now one thing that I feel might be misunderstood here would be, thinking challenges and failures are the same or related, but believe me they are actually not. They are two completely distinct concepts. Also like you might know this book will be incomplete if I will not talk about failures. So that means there is a topic where I will be covering failures and how to overcome them in detail later in the book, since there is a sequence in which I am taking things up.

CHAPTER EIGHT

THINK DIFFERENTLY

Thinking differently/ innovation/creativity is important to be there, at the top.

Have you ever come across that child who gives every single answer in mathematics class and that too in a very short period of time?

Have you ever wondered how he/she is able to do that? Is s/he from mars? Definitely not.

Well the answer is s/he thinks differently, tries putting in that method which will save time.

And when s/he gives the answer every single student in class looks at that child and be like we just finished writing the question. This is actually so relatable for me and might be for you as well.

Everyone wants to be that kid, right? But do you think that he learnt that subject overnight? Also s/he faced failures (getting wrong answers). But it was only that child's hard work, diligence and patience that helped that child to think differently from others.

Now don't worry because I am here to tell you how you can actually think differently to be successful.

You might have noticed that all successful people think differently, and it can be a major game changer.

So to think differently remember to see each and every phase of your lives from different aspects. Think what if you do something totally the other way round. By this I don't mean to drink an apple or eat water. That would be silly.

Also I know most of us nowadays when we see a successful person we try to be in that field, follow his/her footsteps rather than creating our own. We think that if that particular person has achieved success by following those steps we will also surely do so. But instead of being successful we end up being fail and wonder where the things went wrong.

Let me tell you if something works for one person doesn't mean it's going to work for you as well. So let's discuss how we can change our thinking to achieve more.

Now first is to always have that thirst inside you of doing something much bigger than the first time. If you have achieved something, well first congrats, don't think that it's enough for me. Even if you have achieved your ultimate goal, now you might think that I have gone crazy. Like why am I telling you to continue hard work even if you have already achieved what you wanted?

Well see, that is the thinking I am talking about. Now for example your dream was to become an engineer and you did. So what are going to next, take your degree and dance with it every single night, obviously no. You still have to work hard and get yourself a job, even now you will still keep going and work on how you can actually try to get yourself a much better salary. Well if you think getting a salary you never thought of is called success, well then you are wrong. Now you have to think of how you can make an impact on the IT sector so that people can remember you.

This dream might seem too big to be achieved but actually we never work that hard to achieve a dream like this. And it compels us to say at the end, well this was too big to be done. Now everyone can tell you to dream big. But what is the use of dreaming big if we never try to work for that dream.

Now you think that it's easier said than done. Well that's true, achieving something beyond what someone has expected from you takes a lot of hard work and determination.

Well, then did you at least start? Many of you have said no, but some are there with a yes. For all those who said yes tell me what compelled you to think that this is much beyond than I can ever think of achieving.

Did some failures strike your way, or maybe you didn't feel motivated anymore, or 24 hours were not enough for you. Did you know now what that one thing was, which pushed you from hugging your dream, now it's your duty to work for it.

Another important component of thinking differently would be to prioritize things. Well that's obvious because you cannot give more importance to the things that barely take 5 minutes, rather you will work hard for the things that you know are difficult.

So now you know the importance of thinking differently because success requires action and action requires thoughts.

Well before moving on to our next topic I would like to end this one by a quote,

"The people who are crazy enough to think they can change the world are the ones who do."

~Rob Siltanen

CHAPTER NINE

I AM POSSIBLE

Now after listening to the topic you might think that I wrote it incorrectly but tell me have ever tried to read the word impossible this way. In this topic I am going to cover a few points including some tips and tricks which can help you feel that nothing is actually impossible.

You might sometimes think that achieving your goal/dream is impossible. Now I know that you would be able to answer this question yourself at the end.

So let's first consider why we feel like something is impossible with an example.

You are starting your startup and there are chances that a lot of hurdles might come on your way. Are you going to sit down or will you try facing it?

All the successful startups had so many downfalls but today they are the perfect example of turning impossible to "I am possible".

I feel what you listen to is how you act. Let me explain. Suppose you love doing something but the people around you tell you to stop doing it, or you can never do this, or why are you wasting time doing something like this. After getting all these comments your brain will automatically think that maybe I am not worth it. That's when the topic of positive thinking comes up, I have talked about it later in the book.

On the other hand if you will think that, I know I can do this, I am worthy of being where I wanted to be and I will be there. Believe me no can stop you. Because it is just your brain who thinks, which are all those tasks that can be a bit tricky, so tell your lazy brain to start thinking that I can do this. And I will turn impossible into I'm Possible.

There are so many stories that are worth sharing that have done the impossible and believe you are no less, if you also want to be successful then put all your blood and sweat into something. I know the results will not ditch you. Even a small positive thought can make a big difference.

I know everyone tells you the same thing, but then what is the difference between me and other people?

It is that I know that it is just our brain messing around with us and once you have over your thoughts believe me no one stops you from winning the race of life.

Now you might wonder how I can learn to control my brain. Right? Well it is only you, this thing can't be a teacher , it just comes with a lot of experience, knowledge, failures, hard work and focus. Now you might wonder what we learnt. The one major thing you learnt is that our 'brain' is the real reason which is stopping us from getting what we want, but the other part of the lesson is something you will get to know yourself with time. Since you know time is the biggest teacher and the things no one else is capable of teaching us, time does that job.

CHAPTER TEN

NEVER COMPARE YOURSELF

Now it is one of the most important steps that will help you to be at the top. Now you might think that I always say this at the beginning of every topic. Well now you know that each and every topic that I am covering is super important. So, as the title says, do not compare yourself, what do you think it means?

Take time and answer, well most of you might have thought to never compare ourselves with any of our friends or relatives. Because technically we are not the same person, right?

Well your answer was right but I would like to add a second part to it.

Also we don't have to let others' comparisons ruin our self-confidence. I know it might have happened to you at some point of your life when your parents, teacher or maybe some relative have compared you to someone and said, well s/he can actually do much better than you.

And us being us have stuck to that. In situations like these, never let anyone's comparison let you down. They might not know what you are capable of but you know your strengths. From now onwards if you ever get such a comparison from anyone, don't be angry, sad or doubt your skills. Instead, stay quiet and repeat in the back of your mind, "calm down, I know I am good at this and I can do it, maybe not this time, but there is always a next time"

No one is strong enough to break our determination, it's just that we need to make our determination out of diamond, being the hardest rock.

Let me tell you people are always going to be there to back you off and tell you to give up. But you don't have to because you know your capabilities and this is me telling this for, I don't know how many times. I guess I lost track over counts.

It's because I want to make this thing clear and want you to have faith in yourself. Because I am not going back until I can make you reach there, because you can do this, I know.

Everyone is capable of doing great things but not all of them are able to stay till the end of the race. But I promise you that you will be where you are dreaming to be. And I will be standing at the end of the race to congratulate you. After all, it's an achievement.

Like I said everyone is capable of doing great things but most of them aren't because of several reasons like someone doesn't know where to start from, or maybe people back off a few of them, or some don't have a person to guide them through, or some accept their failures. That's why if you don't want to fail,

Don't compare yourself to others,

Because when we see others doing great we always try to follow their footsteps, which is big no things will not come out the same as you have planned them to be. It's better to be your own.

Let's take an example: suppose there is an essay writing competition and you have to take part in it. Now when the jury will receive all the essays I can guarantee you 95% of the ideas are going to be unique, unless someone just posted their essay in a public group.

By this example I want you to understand that everyone has their own identity and they are unique too. So no one is in that position to be able to compare someone.

When a farmer crops his crops, not all the crops end up being the same. So how can we expect some to be the same as the other?

Now I always try to cover both the main things in topics like these, such as how to deal/cure/overcome it and how we can stop/

take steps/prevent what is going on.

We, being a part of society, have to know that if we feel hurt from all those comparisons/hate comments then doesn't it become our duty to stop this since our actions can also hurt someone's feelings.

Now there will be a topic of helping others ahead in the book but for now that's it for this topic. Now before moving on to our next topic I would like to say one last thing, which is, you are doing great to keep up the good work.

CHAPTER ELEVEN

THE 8-8-8 RULE

Now this rule is magical if you want a balanced life. Well you might think what is the role of balanced life in achieving success? Well you know the drill, I am going to explain and give examples and then at the end you will be able to answer this question yourself.

So first let me tell you how this rule actually works.

We all know that we have 24 hours a day.

So this rule splits our 24 hours into three main categories to be productive throughout the day which are as follows.

- Sleep (8 hr)
- Work (8 hr)
- For yourself (8 hr)

So now let's talk about each one of these one by one.

SLEEP

We all know the benefits of getting a good sleep and it is so important to have one. Our working hours shouldn't exceed. You might feel that if I am working way too much it's not going to harm my body or mind. But you are wrong. There are so many diseases that are caused because of lack of sleep including hypertension, obesity, heart attack, diabetes and even depression. Well I don't want you to suffer from any of these diseases, so promise yourself to get a good sleep every day. And even if you have a bad sleeping schedule, try improving it from today.

WORK

Now your work time includes all those things you do throughout the day to prepare for the big day. It could be studying and preparing for an upcoming exam. Now I feel that managing our work time could be a bit tricky but with regular practice and prioritizing things you can be on the track.

LEISURE/FOR YOURSELF

Now some of you might feel that isn't 8 hours a day is too much leisure time. Well let me tell you it includes all the activities ranging from health and hygiene to spending quality time with family and friends and the rest could be utilized for soul purification and eating meals.

Well now you actually know that 8 hr of leisure time isn't too much especially on weekends.

Like I said this rule is magical and I am actually following it for a very long time and the results are amazing. You should follow this rule out since it helps you to be on track and save time. Well there are some days when I end up breaking this rule if I have an important project or an event to prepare for. But then I always get back on track. So don't worry if you break the rule. Obviously we have to manage and balance our lives according to the circumstances.

Well I guess now you know the answer to the question I asked in the beginning of the topic. And yes, balance is so important for achieving success because it helps us to be extra productive and enjoy every single day along with working for our goal.

Also one thing that I would like to say is, take breaks in between. Well you might think that damn we already know this, and it's okay if you do. But I feel like taking breaks in between is super important to freshen up our minds. I know most of you when taking a break might not see yourself studying again unless someone tells you to. So from now onwards be a little organized and please don't check your phones in between a break. You can simply have some fresh air, eat a quick snack, or maybe lie down for a while but please don't sleep.

Taking breaks is important to increase productivity but wasting time and telling it to be a break is like stepping on fire. We only have 24 hours a day and always try to make the most out of it because those 24 hours are never going to come back.

"My brother once told me, "I wish I could get two extra hours a day". I asked him why he needs two extra hours a day? He then told me, I have to do my homework. I was shocked but was laughing from inside. I then asked him to tell where are all those 24 hours of his day going into, and he said, I sleep for 8 hours, meals can be done in 3 hours, I play 4 hours (2hr shift twice), leisure time 5 hours and 4 hours goes into my online classes. I told him okay well, suppose I gave you two extra hours would you be able to complete your homework now and he said, yes! Of course. Well then I told him that no it doesn't really matter if I will give you 2 or 5 extra hours a day. You still will be able to complete your homework because if 24 hours are less for you then, 26 or 29 hours are also not going to be of much help. Because if you actually want to complete your homework you would have done it in those 24 hours only by compromising your sleep or playing time. "I guess my brother learned his lesson and now does his homework on time.

So before moving on to our next topic I would like to say that this topic contains two to three subtopics in itself which could not have been taken individually but hold great significance in itself.

CHAPTER TWELVE

FAILURES

I guess we are on the most important topic of this book right? Failures, what first strikes to your mind when thought of it or I should say, how do you define failures?

Take a moment, ask yourself. Ready, great. Well, let's see if your answer matches mine. I love defining failures to do something much more extraordinary than the first time. Now as I am going to continue with this topic you will get to know why I gave this definition of failures

I feel failures are necessary to spice up our lives a little bit. But the most ironic thing is that people nowadays don't want to see failures in their lives. Life is not like walking on rose petals, there are going to be paths full of spikes and rocks but at the end when you will be on the path on which your dream is waiting to hug you, I know you will feel like all that was worth the joy. Doesn't it sound so great?

Well in this topic I am going to tell why failures occur, and what you can do to move on and do much better next time and don't give yourself a single chance of being failed.

So what according to you could be the reason behind failures? Lack of preparation or maybe some of you might think that luck is an important factor.

Well I will be talking about if luck is one of the factors that influence your failures.

But for now let's talk about how lack of preparation can result in failures.

So let me explain with an example. Imagine that you have your dream in front of you, everything you have ever craved is now being fulfilled. All the name, fame and success is there. Tell me if you are ready to face it. Ask yourself if you are prepared to live that life.

Wait are you terrified, or maybe confused or maybe you are beyond happy to imagine all that.

It doesn't really matter how you feel but the thing that matters the most is you will not be able to handle all that.

Want to know why, okay then. Because you didn't have any failures in your way. Sounds absurd but it's not. Failures are the ones who actually gave us that courage of wearing our crown of success proudly. Let me tell you, success doesn't teach us as much as failures do. So now you know the reason why you would not be able to handle your dream currently. Achieving something requires hard work and determination. If you will achieve what you want without struggling, believe me you will take that thing for granted. Long stories short, “you cannot handle your dream right now”.

Okay now let’s talk about the main thing which is lack of preparation. Most of the people fail because they are not prepared for the circumstances and the challenges that are waiting on the path to stop them from moving any further.

Well most of the people succeed and deceive those failures, while others stick to them.

CHAPTER THIRTEEN

LUCK

So what do you think about luck? Does it really hold significance in making us fail? Is it really one of the factors that we need to keep in mind while aiming for success?

Let me tell you luck is really not that big of a deal when it comes to deciding whether we will be successful or not. And let's assume if it is then what?

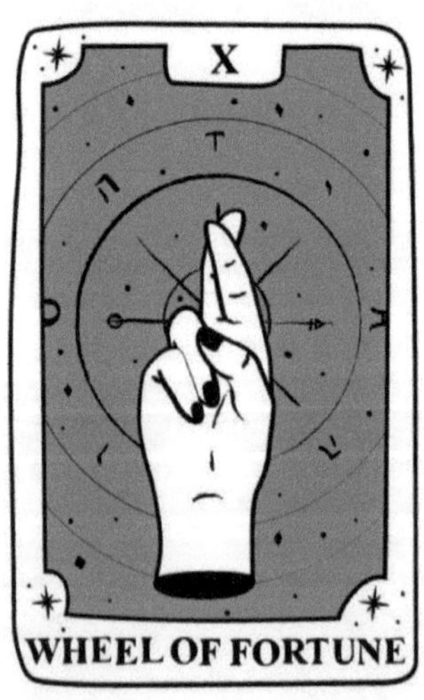

Let me explain with an example, your luck holds 50 % of the reason behind your success and the other factors accounts for the other 50 then let us assume that you cannot have any control over the first 50% so you will probably try your best to get the full control over the second 50% in your hands because all you can do about luck is absolutely nothing.

But the most ironic thing is that when we feel our luck is not favoring us we don't even try to work for the second 50% which totally depends on us and end up failing.

So, this means we cannot say that our luck is not shining the way it usually does. Rather we should say I just don't feel like working anymore for my success. Now tell me will you still blame luck as the factor which hinders your success. You know the answer yourself.

Well that is why I love this dialogue from one of the famous movies and it says, 'Luck favors the prepared'

Okay now in the second scenario let's assume that your luck is favoring you and you sit to give a MCQ test thinking my luck is shining brightly. How much do you think you are going to score? Well fun fact the probability of doing the entire test right is equivalent to becoming the ceo of Google. So I guess that's it. Now you know that it would be useless to blame your luck as the one hindering your success.

Also there are various other small factors that account for our failure that we need to keep in mind like, not taking decisions in a hurry, valuing time, positive thinking and many more.

So now I am going to tell you how you can actually overcome your failures and work hard so you don't fail this time.

First things first, if you are afraid of failures so don't be since they are the third most important teacher after time and challenges. Also having failures is a part of life and there is nothing you can do about them. You cannot change the mistakes that you made in the past , so don't stress thinking about them , rather be prepared so you don't have to regret the same thing in the future.

I know it is hard when failures strike and it seems like all of a sudden our hard work and diligence were for nothing. Now this topic is related to depression about which I have talked earlier as well. This is life not a cake walk but an actual one. Have you ever walked on the sand when it is really hot on a summer day, our feet burn so bad that when we walk down to pour some water on them it feels like yes we make the right decision at the right time. Similarly, whenever you find failures in your life, quickly run and do some hard work to pour the water because then you will feel the same way, that you took that decision at the right time to have a comfortable life ahead.

I know you will work hard because you are capable of doing that. Never look back and I know you will be where you want to be.

CHAPTER FOURTEEN

THINK POSITIVE

Well this is the topic about which we have heard very often in our lives. Everyone knows that thinking positive is important and ultimately brings positive results. We all know this right? We know that just a single positive thought can have a great impact on our mind, body and results.

But ask yourself when was the last time when you thought something really bad the thing you did not want to happen or I should have asked when the last time when negative thoughts popped in your mind was? I know you might say not very often/ recently but deep down you actually know that it actually happens with me. Even though we try hard not to let in all those negative thoughts in our mind but somehow they still squeeze in and find their way in.

In this topic I will be covering a few reasons why we should think positive and telling you a few ways to throw away all the negativity that's stuck at the back of your mind.

Now first let me tell you how positive thinking influences your success. You know the drill, let's take up an example.

So you are taking part in a speech competition and you feel that you are not going to win since you have a strong competitor. Well even if your speech was way better than your competitors you would still lose because your mind has agreed that it's not my cup of my tea. Rather than thinking negatively you could have thought that it doesn't really matter if I have a strong opponent I can still win if I do my best.

Positive thinking actually helps in shaping the outcomes so tell all those negative thoughts to pack up and find a new place since you don't want the outcome/result to be the exact opposite of what you thought to happen.

Also, as much as I do, I focus on always thinking positive but we should remember one thing that we don't have to think/feel the same way when something bad happens to us. If something bad happens in your life don't go around and try to hide your actual emotions, I am not saying to think positive even if a disaster happens in your life. Don't try to manipulate your feelings. Thinking positive in general is a great thing, which is basically what I am trying to say right now.

Also some benefits of thinking positive are lower rates of depression and stress, increase in the life span and the list goes on. Thinking positive can actually help you to increase the percentage of being successful as compared to a person who is not a big fan of positive thinking.

Like I said earlier we all want to think positive but are unable to do so because negative thinking is stubborn. But I know how you can be a strict parent to negative thinking and force it to be grounded for the rest of your lifetime.

There are actually a few ways to do this-

Meditation- Doing any type of meditation can actually help in elucidating all the negative energy from our minds. Now I am not asking you to follow a hardcore routine of doing meditation. You can do it at any time of the day, even meditating for 5 minutes a day can help in bringing great changes and you can eventually increase the time as you get used to it.

Maintaining a gratitude journal- Now I know this is something that actually works fantastically. So if you don't know how to maintain a gratitude journal, I am here. All you need is a diary or any notebook and a pen to write from. Start writing what you are thankful for once a week. Continue doing that for 4 months and you will notice a change, that too a positive one, in your thinking.

Start your day with a positive note- From now onwards tell yourself to think seething positive every day you wake up. Please don't engage yourself in a fight as soon as you wake up. Try starting off your day with something that makes you feel to live that particular day with more excitement.

Also there are small changes that you can make in your life in order to see big ones.

And I always believe that it is good to have changes in yourself by the time it is for your betterment.

Well now you actually know the significance of thinking positive in achieving success and now you also have some tips and tricks that will come handy when you will work to eliminate all the negative thoughts from your mind.

CHAPTER FIFTEEN

SOCIALIZING

Now after talking so much about how society hinders our growth and pushes us back, here I am telling you guys to take part in that society. Isn't this thought conflicting according to you? Well not at all.

First thing I would like to tell you would be not all the people are the same in the society.

So there are basically two kinds of people; first are the ones who are jealous of you, so whenever you surround yourself around these types of people they become angry because they are not accustomed to your success.

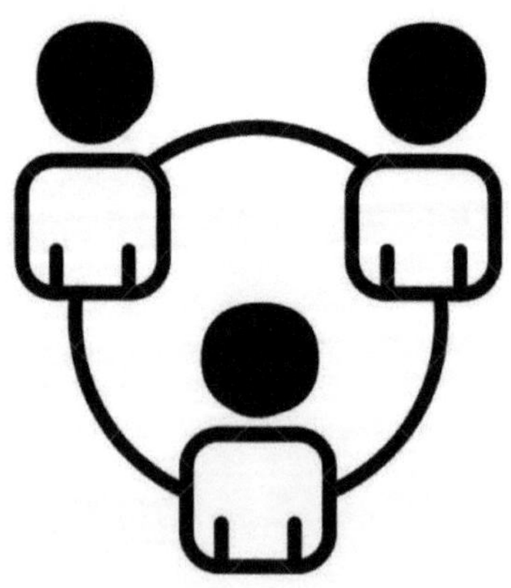

Secondly there are people who genuinely want good for you and are happy for your achievements. So now you know which kind of people you should surround yourself with.

But that's not it, the people who actually criticizes you can be of great help. Wondering how? Well I will be telling that later in the topic.

So let me tell you why it is important to take part in society to be successful.

Well first things first people are important for mental health as well as for social development. You cannot always be in your bubble. You have to come out of it if you want to learn. Life is all about taking lessons and applying them in real life. And those lessons aren't the ones which are available on the internet but you have to search for those life experiences on your own.

Believe me these life lessons are way more important than the ones that were taught in our textbooks.

Okay let me ask you something now, suppose you started your very own business and you actually want to know the areas where your company can improve. Now tell me what you will do in this case.

Probably you are going to take advice from people. But not from your relatives and friends but from the ones who will give an honest one.

Let me explain with an example-

Tata, one of the biggest car manufacturing companies, introduced one of its cars which was the Tata Sumo. Now there is an inspiring story of why this car was given this particular name.

Every day top executives of the company used to have lunch together. But Mr. Sumant Moolgaokar, was never there to have lunch with his colleagues. Instead everyday he used to take his car and ate his lunch in a dhaba (a small roadside food stall). One day his colleagues followed him and they were surprised to see that he was having his lunch with truck drivers in that same dhaba. Mr.

Sumant Moolgaokar used to do that because he asked those truck drivers the limitations of driving a Tata truck, just so he can work on those limitations.

That is the reason Tata named that car in the honor of such a hardworking executive.

The lesson we learnt was if he wanted he could have discussed those limitations in an office meeting as well but instead he actually wanted to see a change.

Remember when I said critic's play an important role in our lives it's because they say the truth we want to hear. They tell you where you are lacking. They can tell you what are all those things you still need to work on, in order to be at the top.

So from now on, when you find such a person, never ever lose them, because ultimately they are going to be the reason behind your success one day.

Taking part in society is also important because it helps you to improve and develop mentally. We all need people in our lives, especially the ones which can make us laugh. Believe it makes a lot of difference if you have someone by your side to talk to, to share your feelings to. So from now on, I will take part in society.

Now it is also very important for our social development. It gives us an idea of how to behave and manage ourselves whenever we are in public. And it is important to learn that since it allows us to live a very formal life. It is important to know how to be among people and ultimately becomes one of the reasons that leads us to success.

Now the question comes how we can take part in society. Well I am here to tell you.

There are literally so many ways which I can state but I will try to state the most common ones that we can actually follow easily.

You can try taking part in your school and college events and do some community service in nearest nonprofits.

It will actually give you a lot of experience, some of the qualities like teamwork, leadership, acceptance and patience. Starting taking small initiatives in your lives can actually help you in making great changes ahead in your life.

Now let's move on to our next topic, I know this journey so far has been great and I know it will be further as well. All I know is that you are doing great and we can do this together.

CHAPTER SIXTEEN

LEARNING FROM OTHERS

This topic holds great significance in it. It is actually so important to be able to learn from others.

Whenever we see a successful person what we do is, we focus on their rising success. What we don't see is there is so much hard work, diligence, focus, passion and desire that goes into the making of a successful life. There are so many failures behind their success but we never try to analyze them.

Believe me making mistakes is not intentional. No one wants to have a life with mistakes in it. But we still make mistakes, why? It's because we are human. But while making mistakes we make another mistake which is, we often forget to learn from it. It is always said to never be afraid of making mistakes and it is true. But what is the use of making mistakes if we are not able to grasp the lesson. Also if you are tense over something you did in the past please don't be because you cannot change your past or can you? So why waste time over thinking something you have absolutely no control over. And that is when I came up with this quote-

"Don't focus on what's gone, focus on what's yet to come"

~Srishti Wadhwa

What we can do right now is learn from the mistakes that others are making. Because believe me learning how to face and tackle problems is so great. It gives you a lot of confidence because you already know what I can do to tackle these types of mistakes. I know we are taught from a young age that mistakes are the only ones that help us to learn in our lives. But the problem is we often forget that we don't have to repeat them again and again.

Always try to learn from the life of others. Believe me there is so much that one can learn in their lifetime and it is impossible to gather all the knowledge that is available out there, even if a person spends 24/7/365 learning. And that is why it is rightly said that life is too short to make the most out of it.

All you have in your hands right now is just a life which you can either waste or you can turn it up into something wonderful that everyone can look up to say that, Yes! This is the kind of life I want.

Now it's not only that you have to try learning from the lives of successful people only. You can also learn so much from the lives of the people that surround you. It's not about the person, it's about whether their mistakes don't matter big or small. All that matters is the lesson that remains with you from a lifetime.

Money is temporary but experience and knowledge is permanent. A person might rob you but s/he will never be able to rob your skills and talents. It's okay if you don't have money, you can convert your knowledge and experience into money. And now you gotta know why I focus so much on learning new things every day.

To be able to learn from others is a blessing and it's not like you would be able to learn so easily how to see every aspect of your life differently. Remember when we talked about how to think differently, I told you then as well that it takes time to know how you can actually see things differently. Let me explain with an example.

Suppose you got into a fight with one of your classmates and s/he is speaking very rudely to you. What will you do in that situation? Probably try being super mean and arrogant to her/him right? No, that's wrong, remember when I talked about spreading love. Instead of being rude to her/him. Try speaking as politely as possible, believe me she might even stop fighting. In this situation we flipped upside down the whole situation and learnt that it is not always right to come back at people, especially when it is something that is not too serious. Some problems can be solved peacefully as well.

But when I say this I don't mean to be beaten by someone thinking why I should get into a fight. I mean you have to do self-defense at that time.

I always tell people to spread love and be peaceful but please don't take it to the next level where people start taking advantage of you because of your innocence. That is also not right.

Now this was a very small example which I told there are so many things I could probably list off.

But let's talk about our main focus here, which is to be able to learn from the lives of other people.

We have a population of 7.7 billion and even though it is impossible to think for a while of what would happen if I try listing what people have learnt throughout their lives.

I can assure you that even if I try writing a book on every person and what they have learnt till now. Believe me there are going to be 7.7 billion books I can write. Which is not possible though.

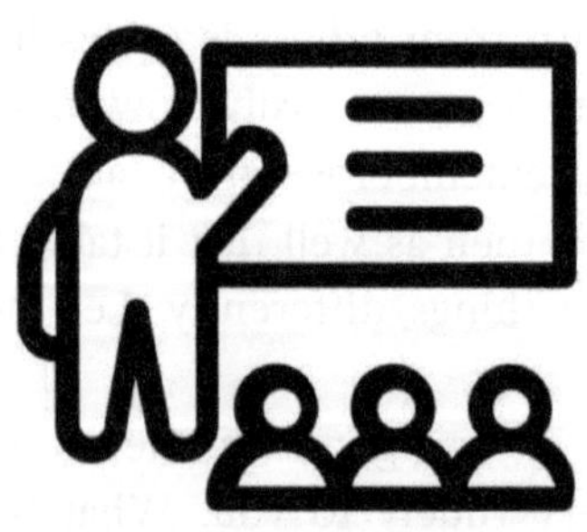

But the thing that I am trying to tell right now is there is so much to learn in this world and what we have is just a life and that too we don't know when we are going to die.

Every person has taken birth and is probably going to die too. So why waste time hating people, being mean. Try learning as many things possible in this lifetime, try different things out whatever comes to your mind, do that, if you feel like snowboarding, do that, if you feel like having your art exhibition, do that, if you feel like dancing, then dance. Because I don't want to regret these things when you will be on your deathbed. Now you might think why I always talk about dark things such as death, depression, suicides. It's because it is the reality and I try to face it. But now it will not only be me facing reality, we will face it together.

If you also want to have that Ferrari, McLaren, Bugatti or Lamborghini standing in your garage then work hard for it. There is now way you can't achieve that. It's just that you have to work hard. I know you can have your dream car, I know you can get into your dream university, I know you can get your dream job, I know you can buy a house that you have always dreamt of, I know you can do this all.

You can, yes you, you are capable of doing this. And you will do this.

Now we are about to move on to our next topic and if you have stuck till now, promise yourself to stick till the end. We are going to do this together.

CHAPTER SEVENTEEN

BEING REALISTIC

We are living in a world of lies. Name that one person who has never spoken a lie. Probably everyone on this earth must have spoken some lies throughout their lifetime, and if you feel you haven't, well you are great.

Ask yourself if you have ever lied to yourself? Now you might wonder how a person can lie to themselves.

Let me explain it with an example. You woke up and started your day. Your entire day passed out doing nothing. And at the end of the day you feel like you had a productive day. So this means you are lying to yourself.

Lying to yourself is the biggest sin that one can do. Believe me it's no one's loss except for yours. Now in this topic I will cover how you can actually be realistic to yourself and how it will help you in achieving your goal.

Now first let me tell you that it's okay if you were not productive someday. But faking yourself is not acceptable. I know there are going to be days where you will feel like doing nothing and that is perfectly fine. But please don't try to be fake productive because it will harm you in the long run.

Now it's not just that we are being fake productive. Like I said in the beginning we are living in a world of lies, I actually meant it, let me explain how. I know most of you reading this might have a social media account. And living in this virtual world is very dangerous.

If you brag of having more followers, listen to me, no one is actually going to help you when you need people, rather everyone will back off as if they don't know you.

We all are so obsessed with posting what we are eating, where we are traveling, I mean it is encouraging us to be in our virtual bubble. And believe me all are trapped inside that bubble and it's our responsibility to pop that bubble and let ourselves free from this bubble full of jealousy, hatred, negativity and fakeness.

Now you might wonder why I am talking about a whole new topic, well it is related, remember when I talked about how taking part in society can help you in achieving success.

Now I think you might find it relatable, we are trying to fake ourselves by living in this virtual world and it ultimately separates us from society. But taking part in society is important for us but by faking ourselves to be in our bubble hinders our success.

Now you see that these two topics are interlinked.

Now let me tell you how you can try not to fake yourself in order to have a better life which will ultimately help you in being successful.

So the first thing is, to have courage to accept your mistakes rather than blaming it on others or telling yourself that it was not your fault.

If you have the courage to accept your mistakes, believe me you are one of the strongest people in the world. And we already know if you know what your mistakes are you can learn from them. So it's basically by doing one thing you are having multiple benefits.

Second thing you can do is know yourself better, what are all those things which you are good at and which things do you need to focus more on. By doing this you will not only start being better at multiple things but it will also help you in being experienced. And you all already know the importance of experience in our lives.

Third thing is to stop pretending. We all know that we are living in a world where people are trying to impersonate different sides of theirs. We always try to be like someone else, why? I truly feel that no one should have any problem with who they really are.

Try accepting who you really are. Believe me it will make a lot of difference. Don't change your habits if someone doesn't like it all about what you like. But one condition here is that the habit should be a good one.

Well these three things will actually help you in being realistic to yourself. And if you feel that it doesn't really hold any significance. Well, then let me tell you. Being who you really are truly makes a lot of difference.

So from now onwards promise yourself to be realistic to yourself. I feel the journey of success also has some points which might not seem important to you but they truly are. There are so many small things apart from the major ones that you need to keep in mind while aiming for success. Because at the end these things will be the only one to help you win the race more efficiently.

CHAPTER EIGHTEEN

ASKING FOR HELP

Have you ever experienced this- you are trying to do something new but you need help for it and your father/mother asks you if you want any help. But you being you says, No! Thanks in vain. And ultimately at the end you go and ask for help for that problem to be solved.

I feel this is actually so relatable. So what is the lesson? Okay! So if I have to tell in one line I would say- "Life could be pretty hard if you try doing everything on your own"

If you are stuck in a situation go ask for help, if you don't know how to do this/that ask for help, if you are confused ask for help, if you feel you can't do this alone ask for help.

Our generation wants to look cool and they think people will think them to be smart if they can do everything on their own. Which is absolutely wrong?

You might think I would be embarrassed asking for help. But that embarrassment comes from inside, right? Then tell yourself it's not wrong to ask for help neither it will hamper your skills. Taking help from theirs actually helps us to do something even better.

I wrote a quote in one of my blogs and it says,

"I know life is hard but we can make it easy if we all are together"

So from now onwards you just don't have to ask for help from others but also you have to help others. I know taking help from others will actually make a lot of difference in improving the outcomes.

Now you might think how taking help from others can be helpful in achieving success. Well I am here to answer this. You see, like I said, taking help from others helps to bring much better outcomes than the same thing when you will try doing it on your own.

Now another question that might be revolving around your mind could be, from whom should I take help? Well for this let me tell you, you can ask for help from almost anyone but the only thing that matters is that person should know what they are dealing with. You can ask for help from your parents, teachers, friends and counselor. Believe me it actually makes a lot of difference.

But we are humans and we are not perfect and this means that there are going to be several things in our lives which can be tricky and you cannot expect yourself to be able to confront every problem that arrives your way. Surely you have to ask for help.

Now you might have listened to your parents and teachers telling you to learn to be independent but here I am telling you guys to ask for help. It is quite obvious that you are not going to ask for help for every single thing. Obviously the problems that need more attention and guidance are the ones which need to be asked for help.

So from onwards tell yourself not to feel shy when it comes to asking for help. And to feel courageous and courteous enough to help the people who are in need.

Now this topic was important to talk about because many people don't help someone thinking that this is not my standard, or some people think of not asking for help, thinking others will consider me to be weak.

But see, it's not about the standard or weakness, rather it's all about the courage to ask for help and to help the ones who actually need it.

When do you think a person asks for help? Because they are so over trying and failing multiple times. So tell me isn't it our responsibility to be able to help such a person who lacks the knowledge that we have in abundance.

So before moving to our next topic I will like to say that, respect everyone, since you never know when you would need someone.

CHAPTER NINETEEN

BE GRATEFUL

Remember when I talked about how writing a gratitude journal can help you to improve more and bring positivity in your life. Well I guess now is the time to talk more about this topic.

Tell me what was the first thing that came to your mind after reading the title? What is probably the motive to include this topic when we want to be successful? Like don't you think that this topic would make more sense after we have achieved what we wanted? Now you know I will magically bring a reason that will convince you that this topic is where it deserves to be.

First things first you necessarily don't need to think that we should only be grateful when we actually have what we wanted. I actually feel completely opposite of it. I feel being grateful should be a part of our lives because we have so many things that so many people don't.

I can give you a proof right now, tell me where you are sitting and reading this book, probably on a chair, a desk or maybe on your bed. Do you know so many people don't even have a bed to sleep on, a chair to sit on and a desk to work on? Tell me now shouldn't you be grateful for what you have. Even if you have access to basic amenities then also you should be grateful because there are so many people who don't even have access to basic amenities.

Now instead of cursing about your life every time. Create a habit to always tell yourself that your life is beautiful. Whenever a thought of, why does this always happen to me comes to your mind.

Tell yourself that it is an opportunity given to you to improve that particular situation. And move ahead. Believe me, life is too short to blame things.

Now you might think what the role of being grateful is and how it helps us to be successful? Well I am here to tell you how it actually helps us to get a much more successful life.

I remember when I was in my middle school there used to be a prayer that we all use to do before eating our lunch and it goes something like this,

"Thank you god for world so sweet,
Thank you god for food we eat,
Thank you god for birds that sing,
Thank you god for everything."

Now these four lines might seem to be just like any other prayer but believe these four lines mean a lot in itself. When I was a kid I wasn't able to understand the point of doing this prayer. But now I actually know what exactly this prayer means and also know the importance of speaking it.

Now I am not going to do a critical analysis of this prayer but I am definitely going to tell you the main message that insisted me to give this prayer as an example of always being thankful.

I feel the teachers and our institutions try their best to tell the kids how important it is to be thankful. But at that point of time we are not able to learn that. And it is nobody's fault because we get to know certain things when they actually happen. Like I said, it's important to have experience and that experience comes with confronting various situations in our lives.

Therefore being grateful at each and every point of your life is great.

And if you feel like you have nothing to be thankful about. Let me tell you that the life you have in your life is already the biggest blessing that one could have.

Also living your entire life being grateful can actually bring a lot of positivity and I have already told all the benefits that come with positive thinking and how it helps us in being successful.

I know you guys reading this might have listened to thanksgiving or some of you might have even celebrated thanksgiving. Well if you don't know about it, let me give you a brief. On this day the family usually has dinner together and they tell everyone what they are thankful for. Which is a great thing. But I feel instead of being thankful just for one day, can't we be thankful for the rest of our lives. Like what a positive impact would it leave on our life? Ah, so inspiring.

From now onwards you not only have to be just thankful but you also have to tell people, who curse their life way too much, how being thankful in general can do wonders.

This topic was the one which most of us don't focus on. We all take our lives for granted. That is why I felt this topic is important because all we have is a single life. And it is our duty to make it as beautiful as possible.

CHAPTER TWENTY

ONE LIFE

Well now I have lost the count over how many times I have said that you have just one life. I want to tell you why I focus so much on this fact.

Well most of you might think why am I talking about such dark things, and moreover earlier I told you to always think positive? You might wonder why I always keep changing sides.

Let me tell you, I feel it's really important to know that we can die any moment, like we make plans 20 years in the future and we don't know if we are going to live or not.

That's the truth, we cannot escape death, but what do I actually mean when I say this line? I meant that we should live everyday as if it is the last one. But by this line I don't mean to go shopping, dine in your favorite restaurant because you can die tomorrow. That would be hilarious. But by this line I actually mean that we should give ourselves time out of our busy lives. Try out everything you have ever dreamt of. Because I don't want you to think that your life wasn't good enough when you are on your deathbed.

The real success in your life would be when you can face life and death fearlessly. I felt this topic is important since no one likes to talk about it. I thought I would, because I have to think differently and stand out from the crowd.

Have you ever imagined how everything can be destroyed within a second and you won't be able to realize that. I don't think there is a thing like the afterlife. All you have is this moment and believe me you would not like to waste that. And let's suppose if there is a thing such as afterlife, I will probably write a book there too, because why not?

Sometimes we get so angry, jealous, arrogant, violent, harsh, selfish and cruel that we often forget that we have just a single life and each and every moment is precious. So please don't waste it reflecting the negative habits instead try to spread love, peace and harmony.

I read somewhere if you want people to remember you forever then there are two things that you can do-

Write something so exceptional that even after 200 years people are excited to read it

Or you can do/achieve something so great that its worth of being written

From now onwards whenever you wake up, instead of checking your social media, thank god that he has given you a whole new day to do something meaningful in your life.

Remember no one cares even if we are dying. Don't waste your time thinking that. Tell yourself that these people are not worthy enough to waste time on.

Let me tell you why you are reading this book right now and have stuck to it till now. Because you also want to make your life meaningful and you also want to be one of the persons whom others can look up to.

Remember when I said every person on this earth can be that person who they think of. But they aren't. Want to know why? Because they waste their life doing something that they are not happy with. That's the reason for saying, do what you love.

Because when you do what you truly love from the bottom of your heart, your brain gets to know that yes this is success for me. Success doesn't come from how much money you earn, it comes from what your passion is.

If I go out and ask people what they think about my level of success? Many of them will say that I am not successful at all, because I am not earning, nor do I have done something great.

But people are not the ones who can decide my level of success. If my brain is happy with what I am doing, if my brain thinks that I am achieving what I wanted. Believe me then, no one's opinion matters to me.

"Because success doesn't comes from what society thinks, it comes from what you think about that"

Believe me this exact line mentioned above is one of the reasons I started writing this book in the first place.

Haters are always going to hate, and you have to just shake it off, just like what Taylor Swift said.

Now you might have seen me mentioning that no one cares even if we die. It is quite obvious that the people who love you will remember you. But in these lines I was talking about society as a whole.

So from now on you know the drill, have to be thankful for the one and only life you have and have to make it meaningful for sure.

Now the relevance of this topic in achieving success is such that, when you start everyday living as if it is your last one, your life becomes much more managed, positive and productive. And these three elements are crucial ones when it comes to achieving success in your life.

Promise yourself to do as directed. And believe me you will see changes yourself and that too positive ones.

And remember it is always good to have a change in yourself by the time it is for your betterment.

CHAPTER TWENTY-ONE

EXTRAS

Now after reading the topic you might wonder what could possibly be in this topic. So let me tell you, in this topic I will cover all the small things that could not have been taken up individually but still hold a great significance in achieving success.

So the first thing is our Marks/Grades. Now this one is for all the people who are still in school/college.

Now if you have grown up in a society like mine, you will probably relate to it. I feel India has those stereotypical people in its roots whereas in other countries it is not that big of a deal. But especially in India people are judged not the basis of their interests and passion but on how much they score.

The question here is does our marks matter? I would say NO. I feel our marks don't really define our capabilities and we should not stress a lot about them. Your marks just test how well you can perform in a test.

But some people might misunderstand with if o

I feel that this saying is true to some extent but not studWell if I have to give a straightforward answer ur marks doesn't matter then there is no need to study. Which is absolutely wrong. I still find people saying on their result day, 'a single sheet of p

Thinking our marks don't matter would be the last taper, and I cannot decide what future things should come to your mind. Even our marks doesn't matter we still have to study because we need to cope up with needs of society.

Now when I said our marks don't matter, I didn't mean that you should stop the hard work. Instead I just wanted to bust a myth according to which your marks are the most important thing. Well obviously you have to keep a good GPA if you want to get into your dream university. No questions for that.

I was trying to talk about it in general and I was just clearing it because I don't want you to think that I didn't mean something.

Well with this, the first subtopic is complete. Now let's talk about the second one.

The second one says, don't overload yourself while preparing your goals for the day. Remember when we talked about preparing a 'to do list' for a day, the most important factor that we have to keep in mind is to not overburden ourselves with the tasks that we have to do throughout the day. Be realistic. Obviously you cannot do everything in a day.

If you do not do so, you will never be able to see all the tasks being completed and believe you will not feel productive at the end of the day. So it's better to keep them realistic.

It might seem like a small thing but it is a major one. Let me tell you how, if you will not overburden yourself, you can easily do the tasks decided for a day, which will make you feel extra productive and give you a lot of mental satisfaction as well.

Gradually when you will become used to you can increase the intensity of your tasks and work accordingly. Yes, so that's it for the second one.

The third subtopic says, No one is perfect.

Believe me no one on this earth is perfect. There is not a single person you can look up to and say, yes s/he is PERFECT. There are some areas where we are not good at. It doesn't mean that we will stick to those only.

Just don't stress out about the things you are not good at. Rather focus on the things which are made for you. Let me give you an example-

So let's assume a person is really good at academics but is horrible when it comes to athletics. What do you think s/he should do? Focus on athletics more or work for academics. Obviously, working more for academics does not only sound right but should actually be implemented as well.

Now let's assume the case of visa-versa. Then the outcome should also have been visa-versa.

Now you know the significance of the line, No one is perfect.

But then you might wonder shouldn't we work for our weakness and try being better at it. Well that is exactly what one should do, but then why not in the above mentioned example.

Because in this case we have already tried that thing out but it doesn't work for us. Whereas if it would have been a case where that student had never tried athletics before, then probably he should have worked for that.

Believe me you can do whatever you want, it's just that you have to be passionate about it.

Well that was it for the third sub topic.

Now let's move to our fourth sub topic which says, 'Don't overthink' I know you might have experienced this as well, at just some point. Whenever we are in a problem we become tense and often have a lot of anxiety. And it's pretty normal because it is how humans react to a problem. But instead of being stuck on a problem and overthinking about it. What you should do is get over it. I am going to tell you a few things that will help you calm down.

But before that let me tell you why overthinking is important to be successful. Well what overthinking does is, it basically stops our brain to think what will be better for us and without that thinking we usually end up making decisions that we regret afterwards. So it is really important to take some crucial decisions of your lives slowly and only after analyzing both the sides of taking that decision. It will help in making better decisions that you will definitely not regret afterwards.

Now let's talk about all those by which we can avoid overthinking-

We basically overthinking in two major scenarios-

First one is when we have a major problem in front of us. All you have to do is give your brain time to make the most appropriate decision.

Second one is when someone comments or says something which we were not expecting. Just don't overthink about it. Sit down, take a deep breath, continue doing that and believe me you will feel a lot relieved. Just don't let your brain think that, why could he/she possibly say that, is it really true, Oh! Does s/he said in the other way, why, why, why?

Take a break and drink some water, don't overthink. Believe it does no good for our brain and health in general.

Believe it might seem like a small thing but because of overthinking/lack of time given to our brain in decision making often results in bad choices.

So from now onwards promise yourself to act calmly in every situation. With this our fourth sub-topic is completed.

So now moving on to our fifth sub-topic which is an important one and it says, 'Being Persistent'

Well if you are reading this book carefully you might remember I have stated this before that

"Persistence is the key to success"

Believe it is only the persistence that gives you the courage to run in this till the very end and achieve what you always wanted to have.

Suppose you have an exam tomorrow and you want to score well. Then you have to be persistent until the process gets over, which means that you have to be persistent in studying and preparing for the exam and you also have to be persistent while writing the exam.

Now you know how persistence plays an important role in being successful. Believe me if you truly want something and if you are persistent in achieving that, no one can actually stop you from doing that. Does matter how much failures, hate and disappointments you face, your persistence will act as a convex mirror and will reflect all that back. It's your shield to be able to fight anyone who comes in your way to success.

Now I guess you got to know the importance that persistence plays in order to make your dreams fulfill. So keep that in your mind and let's move on to the next subtopic.

The next subtopic says, How to accept and overcome rejection. It is really an important one because in our path to success, one of the major hurdles is rejection and therefore it becomes my sole duty to tell you more about them.

Believe me there are going to be several rejections in your way but you don't have to stop. I know you can do this because you deserve to be where you want.

Getting over rejects is just like picking up all the blood and sweat that you put into something. Don't be afraid of getting rejections because they are the only ones which will make you much stronger to fight for what you want.

No one can achieve success without getting rejections in their way. Let me tell you that there are so many people that will take part with you in this race, but it's about who can reach till the end.

You don't have to stop in this race, you don't have to be scared about anything, I believe in you and it doesn't matter if someone else does or not.

Your passion is vulnerable, precious and the most beautiful thing that you can ever ask for. Then work for it. Doesn't matter how many rejections come your way, we can overcome them together. Be prepared so that next time you are capable of not opening the door when rejections will be banging the door and striving their way in.

You can let success in from the back door. Everyone will be surprised because rejections were there but still success found a way to be you. Ah! Doesn't it sound great?

Well now let's discuss how we can overcome the rejections.

So the first thing you have to do as soon as rejection strikes is to check where the things went wrong. This will basically give you an idea of which areas to focus more on.

The second thing you are expected to do is to start preparing so that you don't have to face them next time.

The third thing is to have will power and faith in yourself.

And now lastly you have to give it one more shot.

And if you succeed this time, CONGRATS! , but if not then don't be disheartened. Give it one more try.

If your willpower is strong, believe me even the rejections can give up in front of you.

You can do all these steps to ensure you grab the thing which solely belongs to you. And this is the end of the fifth subtopic.

Now it's time to discuss another subtopic. I know you might be wondering, well that's a lot of subtopics. But like I said in the beginning they might seem short but hold great relevance.

Let me give you an example,

Suppose you are in your class and there is an exam tomorrow. You might wonder, another exam. Well I guess we all must have given some exams in our lives, so just understand the topic clearly, I try to keep it relevant. So let's get back to where we started.

We have an exam tomorrow and the teacher told the average kids in terms of academic performance that you can just go through the notes I gave and that will be sufficient.

But the same teacher tells the intelligent students to revise each and every thing thoroughly just so there is not even a slightest chance of losing marks.

And this is exactly what I am doing right now, I feel you all are intelligent and are capable of achieving what you want. That is the reason I am covering the sub topics, to not leave even a slightest chance of not being successful. I want to be happy when you see your results. And all the hard work will pay off.

So now let me you what the next subtopic is all about, 'Cheat Days'

Now after learning so much ranging from time management to being true to ourselves. I am here telling you guys to cheat. Isn't that hilarious.

Well first let me explain why I felt the need to mention this topic in the first place. Now after working so hard we deserve at least some happiness and a free day that can make us feel that we are living our lives as well.

And therefore comes the cheat day. But that doesn't mean you will do no work for quite a few days and will name it a cheat vacation. That is the least expected thing.

So let me first explain the concept of a cheat day.

You have follow a major thumb rule which says,

Work hard on weekdays and work moderately on weekends. Now you might think this is not what a cheat day looks like. And yes it's not.

This was basically an idea given to you of how your typical week should look like. You have to work really hard for five days. And yes you can decrease your work load on weekends.

And it is fine if you will have a cheat day twice a month and maybe three but not more than that. Because I don't want to let go of all the hard work we have done till now.

So on cheat days, you can do whatever you like. Maybe meeting up with one of your friends, going out, dine in your favorite restaurants. Just to you make you realize that you are living your life as well. It will be advisable to have a cheat day on weekends. Because already you have less things to do and you can manage that.

You can call them a day off or cheat days means the same thing. I used cheat days because it looks catchy. Well now you know that I am not just telling you to work and work only. That's the reason I have included a topic of 'making this journey fun' later in the book. But for now stick here with me to know about more sub topics.

Well now it is the time to discuss our seventh sub-topic. Well that's a great number. I didn't expect them to be this many.

So the next one says, 'Listen everyone but do what you feel is right'.

You see there are going to be a lot of people who try giving you various pieces of advice and will tell you to do the things you would never even dream of doing. But that doesn't mean you are going to disregard them. In situations like these it is always better to listen to everyone, but at the end doing what you feel is right.

If you agree you can do that and if not no one is forcing you actually.

So now let me explain with an example, suppose you are at your friend's house and suddenly your friend's mom starts giving you random advice for what to do next. But that doesn't mean you will tell her to stop. You should listen to everyone's advice regardless of how random it is or whether you need it or not.

Well this does not only make you good in front of them, but also help you to learn something new.

And after carrying that heavy bag full of advice you can choose anyone you like, it doesn't matter if they were a part of that bag or not.

Now you know why I felt the need to mention this topic because in your path you will find so many people like this. And it is better to follow what I just said. Even sometimes I get pissed off when someone doesn't stop giving advice and all I do is relax and take deep breaths but I do listen to them carefully. Because one doesn't know when something can come in handy.

With this the seventh sub-topic is over. And there is good news that only one more sub-topic is left, which I am about to discuss right now.

So this last one says, spending time with your family and friends. Well first of all you might wonder why this topic is even here? How can spending time with my family and friends will help me in achieving success? Okay slow down because I am about to clear all your doubts right now.

But first let me tell you that this topic is so important, like I could have written so much information about it. But I will try my best to sum it up in short.

Spending time with your family and friends does not make you feel good but you actually feel like living your life to the fullest.

Believe me the journey towards success does not only require hard work but also requires the love and support given to you by the people whom you love.

And that is the reason it is really important to spend time with the people who you love. Remember when I will talk about making the journey fun, well I guess now the wait is over because it is the next topic.

Also before moving on let me announce that the sab-topics are officially over. So take a deep breath and stick with me till the very end of this journey.

CHAPTER TWENTY-TWO

HAVING FUN

All this time I have been telling guys to stay focused; stay motivated; manage your time wisely, overcoming failures, depression, and rejection; thinking positive; and all the hard things.

But what about having fun? Well I guess it's the time to tell you more about this.

Remember when I told you-

"All you have in your hands is just a lifetime and it depends on you whether to waste it or make it beautiful, just the way you want it to be."

So isn't it my responsibility to tell you how you can actually make this journey fun? You might have experienced that time flies by especially when we are doing something we like.

So put on a seatbelt because there will be some really fun ways which you are about to know in order to make this journey fun.

The first thing you can do is to never take your passion as a burden. Because if it is a burden for you, believe me you will always be 'forced' to do it. Now you know that is the reason I said in the very beginning- your passion should be something that you love from the bottom of your heart. And if it is then you will never find it to be a burden, instead you will like to do it more often.

The second thing you need to do in order to make this journey fun is to understand yourself. Try knowing yourself better. It will not only help you on making better decisions but will also help in making our life much more easier. So from now on, give time to yourself to understand what I truly want. Because believe me if you are happy with what you are doing then no one else's decision really matter.

'Follow your heart because everyone else can adjust expect for your true ambition'

~Srishti Wadhwa

The third thing is to surround yourself with such people who are happy to see your success. Believe me you will find so many people who are not accustomed to your success and they are not of any use. Because the people who stick with you even if you have nothing are the ones who truly deserve to be there when you have everything. There are going to be people who will show up at success like you owe them something but it's better to get rid of such people in the first place so you don't have to regret afterwards.

The fourth thing that should be kept in mind to aim for a happy journey is to know that no one is perfect.

Think of the person whom you admire the most and want to be like. Analyze their life and you will know that there are going to be certain things in which even they are not good at. And now you know that no one is perfect. Don't focus on the things you are not good at instead focus on the things you are good at because believe me life is too short to make the most out of it.

You see when we go on a trip we pack our things accordingly and specially the basic necessities and the ones which will make this journey of yours even more fun.

Well now you know I am right there telling you what all things to pack in order to make it the best journey of your life.

And believe me, I will ensure that you don't forget something because after all I have promised you to make your journey successful. And I will not let you back off and even I will stay till the very end and will watch your airplane successfully taking off.

But wait, this isn't the final goodbye yet. We have a lot more to pack. So continue reading if you want to find out what goes into your suitcase next.

But for now it is the end for this topic and let's move on to our next one.

CHAPTER TWENTY-THREE

HARD WORK

Well, well, well, it might seem a bit too late for this topic to show up. But this book would have been useless if I hadn't talked about hard work.

Two days ago I asked my mother, father and brother to take a sheet of paper and write three things they feel are necessary in order to be successful.

And when I got all three papers, to my surprise the one most common thing that showed up in every list was hard work. And my brother literally filled in all the three spots with hard work.

I sat down and wondered if doing hard work was the only thing that one has to do in order to be successful. But the answer is no, because then why would I name these 24 ways to success?

Also I wondered if doing hard work was really that important. Well the answer is yes, it plays a major role in shaping our success.

But then why am I taking up this topic in the end, if it is that important. It's because to make sure that you don't miss the most important thing when you will be starting this journey.

Well then come on and let me tell you of how you can do hard work in order to be there, the place you always wanted to have. Doesn't it seem like a fairy tale? All our dreams will be coming true. But in this fairy tale, there will be no fairy who can swerve her wand around and will get you whatever you want. You will be the only one doing all that it takes to be where you want to. And I know you deserve to be there, so all you have to do is work hard and do everything you can in your control just to ensure, no one can ever snatch that place away from you.

It's said that- 'Hard work is the key to Success' in fact I totally agree.

So when I say that, it is the hard work that will help you get there, it basically includes everything. You see it includes, exploring your passion, working for your passion, planning it out, knowing your goal, time management, staying motivated, taking challenges, thinking differently, doing the impossible, never comparing yourself , following the 8-8-8 rule, overcoming depression, failures, thinking positive, taking part in society, learning from others, being realistic, going ask for help, living your life, extras, stop multitasking.

And now you know the importance of talking about this topic in the end because you have to do hard work in each one of those to change from dream to real. Hard work means to follow the thing you love from all your heart and putting your life into it.

Whenever you feel like giving up, tell yourself to work hard because it is ultimately going to pay you back. If you had a busy day don't think of the stress you have in your mind, tell yourself that it will happen one day and my hard work will definitely pay me back. Yes, it will and that will be the most beautiful day.

So tell your lazy self not to waste time cozying up in bed, instead stand up to build your future. Utilize the only time you have, and invest it. Believe me you will not regret it.

Well I guess now you know that hard work really is important to be where you want. And with this being said let's move on towards the end. Well it is not the end of our journey yet but our destination is near.

Printed by Libri Plureos GmbH in Hamburg,
Germany